EMMANUEL JOSEPH

The Silicon Sheikhs and Steel Tycoons, Billionaires Who Built Countries

Copyright © 2025 by Emmanuel Joseph

All rights reserved. No part of this publication may be reproduced, stored or transmitted in any form or by any means, electronic, mechanical, photocopying, recording, scanning, or otherwise without written permission from the publisher. It is illegal to copy this book, post it to a website, or distribute it by any other means without permission.

First edition

This book was professionally typeset on Reedsy.
Find out more at reedsy.com

Contents

1. Chapter 1: The Dawn of Ambition — 1
2. Chapter 2: Foundations of Empires — 3
3. Chapter 3: The Tech Boom and Its Titans — 5
4. Chapter 4: Innovating the Future — 7
5. Chapter 5: Industrial Titans and Their Legacy — 9
6. Chapter 6: Bridging the Gap — 11
7. Chapter 7: Pioneering Green Industries — 13
8. Chapter 8: Building the Future of Transportation — 15
9. Chapter 9: Digital Economies and Global Impact — 17
10. Chapter 10: Philanthropy and Social Impact — 19
11. Chapter 11: Leadership and Influence — 21
12. Chapter 12: Navigating Crises — 23
13. Chapter 13: The Power of Collaboration — 25
14. Chapter 14: Legacy and Impact — 27
15. Chapter 15: Reshaping Education — 29
16. Chapter 16: Driving Global Connectivity — 31
17. Chapter 17: The Future of Innovation — 33

1

Chapter 1: The Dawn of Ambition

At the heart of every empire lies the tale of an ambitious individual who dared to dream beyond the ordinary. The narrative of the Silicon Sheikhs and Steel Tycoons begins with such pioneers—visionaries who perceived potential where others saw barren landscapes. Early on, these entrepreneurs faced insurmountable odds, from a lack of resources to societal skepticism. Yet, their unwavering determination forged paths that would later become the foundation of nations. They weren't mere businessmen; they were architects of a new era.

These titans of industry possessed a unique ability to marry ambition with innovation. The Silicon Sheikhs of the tech world transformed silicon chips into the currency of the future, building digital kingdoms that spanned continents. On the other hand, the Steel Tycoons laid the infrastructure that propelled industrial revolutions. Their factories belched the smoke of progress, signaling the dawn of modernity. Together, these leaders redefined the boundaries of possibility, showing that true power lay not just in wealth, but in the ability to transform society.

The journey wasn't straightforward. For every triumph, there were countless setbacks—failed ventures, economic depressions, and fierce competition. These experiences didn't deter them; they refined their resolve. The Silicon Sheikhs faced the rapidly evolving landscape of technology, where today's innovation could become tomorrow's obsolescence. The Steel Tycoons contended with labor strikes, environmental concerns, and the challenge of maintaining quality at scale. Yet, it was through these trials that their legacies were forged.

Their stories are not just about financial success but about the indomitable human spirit. These individuals epitomized resilience and ingenuity, teaching future generations that greatness is born from perseverance and vision. They became symbols of what one could achieve with the right blend of passion, intelligence, and grit. Their legacies continue to inspire, proving that the world isn't changed by the timid, but by those bold enough to chase monumental dreams.

2

Chapter 2: Foundations of Empires

The empires built by the Silicon Sheikhs and Steel Tycoons didn't spring up overnight. They were the result of meticulous planning, calculated risks, and a deep understanding of market dynamics. The early days were marked by small, strategic steps—acquiring key patents, forming alliances, and securing initial funding. These foundational moves set the stage for exponential growth, allowing these visionaries to lay the groundwork for their monumental enterprises.

One critical aspect was their ability to identify and harness emerging trends. The Silicon Sheikhs, with their innate understanding of technology, were quick to recognize the potential of the internet, mobile computing, and artificial intelligence. They invested heavily in research and development, ensuring they stayed ahead of the curve. The Steel Tycoons, on the other hand, capitalized on the burgeoning demand for infrastructure, supplying the steel that would build skyscrapers, bridges, and railroads across the globe.

Their success wasn't solely due to their business acumen; it was also a product of their leadership qualities. They were masterful communicators, able to inspire their teams and rally support from stakeholders. Their vision wasn't just about profit—it was about creating something enduring, something that would outlast them and continue to drive progress. This long-term perspective allowed them to make bold decisions, investing in projects that wouldn't yield immediate returns but promised significant future gains.

Despite their successes, they remained grounded in the understanding that empires are built on the backs of many. They prioritized creating supportive, inclusive work environments where innovation could thrive. By fostering a culture of collaboration and continuous improvement, they ensured that their companies remained at the forefront of their respective industries. Their ability to blend strategic foresight with compassionate leadership became a hallmark of their enduring legacies.

3

Chapter 3: The Tech Boom and Its Titans

The late 20th and early 21st centuries witnessed an unprecedented boom in technology, and at the forefront of this revolution were the Silicon Sheikhs. These tech titans recognized early on that the digital age was not a fleeting trend but a transformative force that would reshape every aspect of human life. They were not just participants in this boom—they were its architects, driving innovations that connected the world in ways previously unimaginable.

Their journey began in humble garages and small labs, where they tinkered with circuits and code, driven by a passion for discovery. The first wave of the tech boom saw the rise of personal computing, with pioneers like Bill Gates and Steve Jobs leading the charge. They democratized technology, making it accessible to the masses and setting the stage for the digital revolution. Their relentless pursuit of excellence and their refusal to settle for anything less than groundbreaking innovations set a high bar for future tech entrepreneurs.

As the internet emerged as a powerful tool for communication and commerce, a new generation of Silicon Sheikhs took the reins. Visionaries like Jeff Bezos, Larry Page, and Sergey Brin saw the internet's potential to revolutionize industries from retail to information search. They built platforms that became indispensable parts of daily life, changing how people shop, search for information, and connect with each other. Their companies grew at a staggering pace, driven by their ability to foresee and capitalize on shifting technological trends.

The tech boom wasn't just about creating new gadgets or services; it was about reimagining how the world works. The Silicon Sheikhs leveraged their platforms to solve complex problems, from improving healthcare with wearable technology to enabling remote work and education. Their innovations have had far-reaching impacts, touching every corner of the globe and transforming societies. They demonstrated that technology could be a powerful force for good, driving progress and creating opportunities for millions.

4

Chapter 4: Innovating the Future

The Silicon Sheikhs weren't content with merely riding the wave of existing technologies; they were committed to shaping the future. This forward-thinking mindset drove them to explore emerging fields such as artificial intelligence, biotechnology, and renewable energy. They believed in the power of technology to address global challenges and improve the quality of life for people around the world. Their investments in these cutting-edge areas laid the groundwork for future breakthroughs and ensured that their companies remained at the forefront of innovation.

Artificial intelligence (AI) became a key focus for many Silicon Sheikhs. They envisioned a world where AI could revolutionize industries, from healthcare to transportation. By investing in AI research and development, they aimed to create intelligent systems that could analyze vast amounts of data, make accurate predictions, and automate complex tasks. The potential applications were limitless, and their efforts in this field led to significant advancements in machine learning, natural language processing, and robotics.

Biotechnology also captured the imagination of these tech pioneers. They saw the potential for biotechnology to revolutionize medicine, agriculture, and environmental conservation. Through strategic partnerships and investments, they supported groundbreaking research in genomics, synthetic biology, and personalized medicine. Their efforts contributed to the development of new treatments for diseases, genetically modified crops with increased yields, and sustainable solutions for environmental challenges.

Renewable energy was another area where the Silicon Sheikhs made a significant impact. Recognizing the urgent need to transition away from fossil fuels, they invested in solar, wind, and other renewable energy technologies. Their commitment to sustainability not only helped reduce carbon emissions but also spurred economic growth by creating new industries and jobs. Their vision of a cleaner, greener future inspired others to follow suit, leading to a global shift towards renewable energy sources.

5

Chapter 5: Industrial Titans and Their Legacy

While the Silicon Sheikhs were transforming the digital landscape, the Steel Tycoons were building the physical infrastructure that would support this new era. These industrial titans understood that a strong foundation was essential for economic growth and societal progress. They invested heavily in the development of steel production facilities, ensuring a steady supply of high-quality steel for construction, manufacturing, and transportation projects.

The Steel Tycoons were instrumental in the creation of modern cities. Their steel beams and girders formed the skeletons of skyscrapers, bridges, and highways, enabling the rapid urbanization that characterized the 20th century. They played a crucial role in the development of iconic structures such as the Golden Gate Bridge, the Empire State Building, and the Burj Khalifa. These achievements not only showcased their engineering prowess but also symbolized the power of human ingenuity.

Beyond their contributions to construction, the Steel Tycoons also revolutionized the manufacturing sector. Their innovations in steel production techniques, such as the Bessemer process and electric arc furnaces, increased efficiency and reduced costs. This allowed for the mass production of automobiles, appliances, and other consumer goods, making them more accessible to the general public. Their efforts helped fuel the rise of the middle class and contributed to the economic prosperity of their respective countries.

The legacy of the Steel Tycoons extends beyond their industrial achievements. They were also philanthropists who believed in giving back to society. Many of them established foundations and charitable organizations that supported education, healthcare, and the arts. Their generosity had a lasting impact on their communities, creating opportunities for future generations and fostering a culture of philanthropy. Their story is a testament to the enduring power of vision, determination, and the belief that industry can be a force for good.

6

Chapter 6: Bridging the Gap

The worlds of the Silicon Sheikhs and Steel Tycoons were initially distinct, each focused on their respective domains. However, as technology and industry evolved, these two spheres began to intersect. The rise of smart cities, autonomous vehicles, and advanced manufacturing techniques required a seamless integration of digital and physical infrastructure. This convergence presented new opportunities for collaboration and innovation, bridging the gap between the digital and industrial realms.

One notable example of this convergence is the development of smart cities. Silicon Sheikhs and Steel Tycoons joined forces to create urban environments that leveraged cutting-edge technology to improve efficiency, sustainability, and quality of life. They integrated sensors, data analytics, and automation into the urban fabric, enabling real-time monitoring and management of resources such as energy, water, and transportation. This holistic approach to city planning transformed traditional urban centers into intelligent ecosystems that could adapt to the needs of their inhabitants.

Autonomous vehicles represented another area where the worlds of the Silicon Sheikhs and Steel Tycoons overlapped. Tech giants invested in developing the software and artificial intelligence needed to navigate self-driving cars, while industrial leaders provided the expertise and resources to manufacture these advanced vehicles at scale. The collaboration resulted in safer, more efficient transportation systems that reduced traffic congestion, lowered emissions, and increased mobility for people of all ages and abilities.

Advanced manufacturing techniques also benefited from the synergy between the digital and industrial realms. Technologies such as 3D printing, robotics, and the Internet of Things (IoT) revolutionized traditional manufacturing processes, making them more flexible, efficient, and cost-effective. Silicon Sheikhs provided the digital tools and platforms that enabled these innovations, while Steel Tycoons supplied the materials and infrastructure needed to bring them to life. This partnership accelerated the development and adoption of next-generation manufacturing technologies, driving economic growth and fostering a new era of industrial innovation.

7

Chapter 7: Pioneering Green Industries

As global awareness of environmental issues grew, the Silicon Sheikhs and Steel Tycoons turned their attention to pioneering green industries. They understood that sustainability was not just a moral imperative but also a significant business opportunity. By investing in clean technologies and eco-friendly practices, they aimed to reduce the environmental impact of their operations while creating new markets and revenue streams.

The Silicon Sheikhs played a key role in the development of renewable energy technologies. They funded research and development in solar, wind, and hydropower, leading to significant advancements in efficiency and cost-effectiveness. Companies like Tesla, led by visionary Elon Musk, revolutionized the electric vehicle industry, proving that clean transportation could be both practical and desirable. These efforts helped accelerate the transition to a low-carbon economy, setting the stage for a sustainable future.

The Steel Tycoons also embraced green technologies, focusing on reducing the environmental footprint of their operations. They invested in cleaner production methods, such as using electric arc furnaces powered by renewable energy instead of traditional blast furnaces. They also explored innovative ways to recycle and repurpose steel, minimizing waste and conserving resources. By prioritizing sustainability, they demonstrated that heavy industry could be compatible with environmental stewardship.

In addition to their contributions to clean energy and sustainable manufacturing, the Silicon Sheikhs and Steel Tycoons supported initiatives to combat climate change and protect natural resources. They funded projects aimed at reforestation, conservation, and sustainable agriculture, recognizing the importance of preserving the planet for future generations. Their commitment to green industries not only helped mitigate the effects of climate change but also inspired others to take action, fostering a global movement towards environmental responsibility.

8

Chapter 8: Building the Future of Transportation

The Silicon Sheikhs and Steel Tycoons played a pivotal role in shaping the future of transportation. They recognized that efficient, sustainable, and innovative transportation systems were essential for economic growth and societal progress. By leveraging their expertise and resources, they developed groundbreaking technologies and infrastructure that revolutionized how people and goods moved around the world.

One of the most significant advancements in transportation came from the development of electric vehicles (EVs). The Silicon Sheikhs, with their focus on clean energy and cutting-edge technology, spearheaded the EV revolution. Companies like Tesla, founded by Elon Musk, created high-performance electric cars that rivaled traditional gasoline-powered vehicles in terms of range, speed, and style. The widespread adoption of EVs helped reduce carbon emissions and dependence on fossil fuels, paving the way for a more sustainable future.

The Steel Tycoons also contributed to the future of transportation by building the infrastructure needed to support new modes of travel. They invested in the construction of high-speed rail networks, which provided a fast, efficient, and environmentally friendly alternative to air and road travel. These rail systems connected major cities and regions, facilitating commerce, tourism, and cultural exchange. The Steel Tycoons' expertise in large-scale construction projects ensured that these ambitious undertakings were completed on time and within budget.

Another area where the Silicon Sheikhs and Steel Tycoons made a significant impact was in the development of autonomous vehicles. By combining advances in artificial intelligence, machine learning, and sensor technology, they created self-driving cars and trucks that had the potential to revolutionize transportation. These autonomous vehicles promised to improve safety, reduce traffic congestion, and increase the efficiency of freight and passenger transport. The collaboration between tech innovators and industrial leaders accelerated the adoption of these technologies, bringing the future of transportation closer to reality.

9

Chapter 9: Digital Economies and Global Impact

The rise of digital economies transformed the global economic landscape, and the Silicon Sheikhs were at the forefront of this revolution. They recognized the potential of the internet and digital technologies to create new business models, streamline operations, and connect markets in ways that were previously unimaginable. By harnessing the power of the digital economy, they built companies that became global powerhouses, driving economic growth and reshaping industries.

E-commerce was one of the most significant developments in the digital economy. Visionaries like Jeff Bezos, the founder of Amazon, revolutionized the retail industry by creating online platforms that allowed consumers to shop from the comfort of their homes. E-commerce giants leveraged data analytics, logistics, and digital marketing to provide personalized shopping experiences and efficient delivery services. Their success not only transformed the retail landscape but also created new opportunities for small businesses and entrepreneurs worldwide.

The Silicon Sheikhs also played a crucial role in the development of digital payment systems. They recognized that secure, convenient, and efficient payment methods were essential for the growth of online commerce. Companies like PayPal, founded by Elon Musk and others, created platforms that allowed consumers and businesses to transact seamlessly across borders. These digital payment systems facilitated the growth of the gig economy, enabling freelancers and remote workers to participate in the global marketplace.

The global impact of the digital economy extended beyond commerce and finance. The Silicon Sheikhs used their platforms to promote social causes, raise awareness about important issues, and drive positive change. Social media platforms, search engines, and digital content providers became powerful tools for communication, education, and activism. By leveraging their reach and influence, the Silicon Sheikhs helped create a more connected and informed world, where information and opportunities were accessible to all.

10

Chapter 10: Philanthropy and Social Impact

While the Silicon Sheikhs and Steel Tycoons amassed great wealth, they also recognized the importance of giving back to society. Philanthropy became a cornerstone of their legacies, as they used their resources to address pressing social issues and improve the lives of people around the world. Their commitment to social impact demonstrated that true success was not measured solely by financial gain but by the positive change one could create.

Education was a primary focus of their philanthropic efforts. The Silicon Sheikhs, in particular, understood the transformative power of technology in education. They funded initiatives to provide access to quality education for underserved communities, develop innovative learning tools, and support research in science, technology, engineering, and mathematics (STEM). By investing in education, they aimed to equip the next generation with the skills and knowledge needed to thrive in a rapidly changing world.

Healthcare was another area where their philanthropy made a significant impact. The Steel Tycoons, recognizing the importance of public health, funded the construction of hospitals, clinics, and medical research centers. They also supported initiatives to combat diseases, improve maternal and child health, and expand access to healthcare services in underserved regions.

Their contributions helped save countless lives and improved the overall well-being of communities.

The Silicon Sheikhs and Steel Tycoons also championed environmental causes. They funded projects aimed at preserving natural resources, protecting endangered species, and promoting sustainable practices. Their support for environmental conservation reflected their commitment to safeguarding the planet for future generations. By leveraging their influence and resources, they inspired others to join the fight against climate change and environmental degradation.

11

Chapter 11: Leadership and Influence

Leadership was a defining characteristic of the Silicon Sheikhs and Steel Tycoons. Their ability to inspire, motivate, and guide their teams played a crucial role in their success. They understood that great leaders are not just those who give orders, but those who lead by example, foster a positive work environment, and empower others to achieve their full potential. Their leadership styles varied, but they all shared a commitment to excellence, innovation, and integrity.

The Silicon Sheikhs were often characterized by their visionary leadership. They had a unique ability to see the bigger picture and anticipate future trends. This foresight allowed them to make bold decisions and take calculated risks that ultimately paid off. They were also effective communicators, able to articulate their vision and rally support from employees, investors, and customers. Their passion for technology and innovation was infectious, creating a culture of enthusiasm and creativity within their organizations.

The Steel Tycoons, on the other hand, were known for their hands-on leadership approach. They often spent time on the factory floors, working alongside their employees and gaining a deep understanding of the production process. This hands-on approach not only earned them the respect and loyalty of their workers but also allowed them to identify and address potential issues before they became major problems. Their pragmatic leadership style ensured that their companies operated efficiently and maintained high standards of quality.

Both the Silicon Sheikhs and Steel Tycoons recognized the importance of investing in their people. They provided opportunities for professional development, encouraged continuous learning, and created supportive work environments. By valuing their employees and fostering a culture of collaboration and innovation, they built strong, resilient organizations that were capable of adapting to changing market conditions and driving sustained growth.

12

Chapter 12: Navigating Crises

The paths to success for the Silicon Sheikhs and Steel Tycoons were not without obstacles. They faced numerous crises, from economic recessions and market crashes to technological disruptions and environmental challenges. However, their ability to navigate these crises with resilience and adaptability was a testament to their exceptional leadership and strategic thinking. They turned adversity into opportunity, emerging stronger and more innovative.

One of the most significant crises faced by the Silicon Sheikhs was the dot-com bubble burst in the early 2000s. Many tech companies saw their valuations plummet, and numerous startups went bankrupt. However, the true visionaries remained steadfast, focusing on long-term growth rather than short-term gains. They restructured their companies, cut costs, and invested in core technologies that would drive future success. Their perseverance paid off, as they emerged from the crisis with stronger, more sustainable business models.

The Steel Tycoons also faced their share of challenges, particularly during economic downturns and periods of industrial decline. Global competition, rising production costs, and environmental regulations posed significant threats to their businesses. Yet, these industrial leaders were adept at identifying and implementing strategic solutions. They diversified their operations, invested in new technologies, and embraced sustainable practices.

By doing so, they ensured the continued relevance and profitability of their companies.

Both the Silicon Sheikhs and Steel Tycoons demonstrated remarkable crisis management skills. They maintained clear communication with their stakeholders, provided reassurance and guidance to their employees, and made tough decisions with conviction. Their ability to stay calm under pressure and make informed decisions helped them navigate turbulent times and position their companies for future growth. Their experiences serve as valuable lessons for future generations of leaders, highlighting the importance of resilience, adaptability, and strategic thinking.

13

Chapter 13: The Power of Collaboration

Collaboration was a key factor in the success of the Silicon Sheikhs and Steel Tycoons. They understood that no individual or company could achieve greatness in isolation. By forming strategic partnerships and alliances, they were able to leverage complementary strengths, share resources, and achieve common goals. Their collaborative approach not only accelerated innovation but also created synergies that amplified their impact on the world.

In the tech industry, collaboration often took the form of strategic acquisitions and partnerships. The Silicon Sheikhs acquired promising startups and integrated their technologies and talent into their organizations. This approach allowed them to stay at the forefront of innovation and quickly adapt to emerging trends. They also formed alliances with other tech companies, research institutions, and government agencies to tackle complex challenges and drive industry-wide advancements.

The Steel Tycoons, on the other hand, collaborated with various stakeholders across the supply chain. They worked closely with suppliers, customers, and industry associations to optimize production processes, improve product quality, and ensure timely delivery. By fostering strong relationships with their partners, they created a resilient and efficient supply chain that could withstand market fluctuations and disruptions. Their collaborative efforts contributed to the overall strength and stability of the industrial sector.

Collaboration extended beyond business partnerships. The Silicon Sheikhs and Steel Tycoons also engaged in cross-industry collaborations to address global challenges. They joined forces to promote sustainability, support education and healthcare initiatives, and drive economic development. By working together, they were able to pool their resources and expertise to create lasting positive change. Their collaborative approach demonstrated that the collective power of individuals and organizations could achieve far more than any single entity could alone.

14

Chapter 14: Legacy and Impact

The legacies of the Silicon Sheikhs and Steel Tycoons extend far beyond their business achievements. They have left an indelible mark on the world, transforming industries, shaping economies, and improving the quality of life for countless individuals. Their impact can be seen in the skyscrapers that define city skylines, the digital platforms that connect people across the globe, and the sustainable practices that protect the environment.

One of the most significant aspects of their legacy is the inspiration they provide to future generations of entrepreneurs and leaders. Their stories of ambition, innovation, and resilience serve as powerful examples of what can be achieved with vision, determination, and hard work. They have shown that true success is not just about financial wealth but about creating lasting positive change and leaving the world a better place.

Their philanthropic efforts have also had a profound impact on society. The foundations and charitable organizations they established continue to support education, healthcare, and environmental initiatives, creating opportunities and improving lives. Their generosity has inspired others to follow in their footsteps, fostering a culture of giving and social responsibility.

The Silicon Sheikhs and Steel Tycoons have also played a crucial role in shaping the future. By investing in cutting-edge technologies, sustainable practices, and innovative solutions, they have paved the way for continued progress and development. Their contributions have created a foundation for future generations to build upon, ensuring that their legacy of innovation and impact will endure for years to come.

15

Chapter 15: Reshaping Education

Education has always been a cornerstone of progress, and the Silicon Sheikhs and Steel Tycoons understood its transformative power. They invested heavily in reshaping the education system to ensure that future generations were equipped with the knowledge and skills needed to thrive in a rapidly changing world. Their initiatives focused on promoting STEM education, integrating technology into the classroom, and supporting lifelong learning.

The Silicon Sheikhs, in particular, recognized the potential of technology to revolutionize education. They funded the development of innovative educational tools and platforms that made learning more interactive, engaging, and accessible. Online learning platforms, such as Khan Academy and Coursera, provided high-quality educational content to millions of students worldwide. These platforms democratized education, breaking down barriers to access and enabling learners from all backgrounds to pursue their academic goals.

In addition to supporting online education, the Silicon Sheikhs also invested in initiatives to bring technology into traditional classrooms. They provided funding for schools to acquire computers, tablets, and other digital devices, ensuring that students had access to the tools they needed to succeed in the digital age. They also supported teacher training programs to help educators integrate technology into their teaching practices effectively. By promoting digital literacy and fostering a culture of innovation, they prepared students for the demands of the 21st-century workforce.

The Steel Tycoons also played a significant role in reshaping education. They funded the construction of schools, colleges, and universities, providing students with state-of-the-art facilities and resources. They supported vocational training programs that equipped individuals with the practical skills needed for careers in manufacturing, engineering, and other industrial fields. By investing in education, they not only created opportunities for individuals to improve their lives but also ensured a steady supply of skilled workers for their industries.

16

Chapter 16: Driving Global Connectivity

One of the most profound impacts of the Silicon Sheikhs and Steel Tycoons was their role in driving global connectivity. They recognized that a connected world was essential for economic growth, cultural exchange, and social progress. By investing in infrastructure and technology that bridged geographical and cultural divides, they created a more interconnected and interdependent world.

The Silicon Sheikhs were instrumental in the development of the internet and telecommunications infrastructure that connected people across the globe. They funded the construction of undersea cables, satellite networks, and data centers that formed the backbone of the digital economy. Their investments ensured that even the most remote regions had access to reliable internet connectivity, enabling individuals and businesses to participate in the global marketplace. The rise of social media platforms, search engines, and cloud computing further enhanced global connectivity, transforming how people communicated, collaborated, and conducted business.

The Steel Tycoons also contributed to global connectivity through their investments in transportation infrastructure. They built railways, highways, and ports that facilitated the movement of goods and people across borders. These transportation networks reduced travel times, lowered costs, and increased trade, driving economic growth and fostering international cooperation. The Steel Tycoons' contributions to infrastructure development were essential for creating a connected and integrated global economy.

The combined efforts of the Silicon Sheikhs and Steel Tycoons created a world where information, ideas, and resources could flow freely across borders. This global connectivity enabled innovation to spread more rapidly, facilitated cultural exchange, and promoted mutual understanding. Their vision of a connected world has had a lasting impact on how we live, work, and interact, bringing us closer together and creating new opportunities for collaboration and progress.

17

Chapter 17: The Future of Innovation

As we look to the future, the legacy of the Silicon Sheikhs and Steel Tycoons continues to shape the trajectory of innovation. Their contributions have laid the foundation for continued progress, inspiring future generations to push the boundaries of what is possible. The future of innovation will be driven by the same principles that guided these visionary leaders: ambition, resilience, collaboration, and a commitment to creating positive change.

One area with tremendous potential for future innovation is artificial intelligence (AI). The Silicon Sheikhs have already made significant strides in AI research, and the possibilities for its application are vast. From healthcare and education to transportation and entertainment, AI has the potential to revolutionize industries and improve the quality of life for people around the world. By continuing to invest in AI and other emerging technologies, future innovators can build on the foundations laid by the Silicon Sheikhs and drive progress in new and exciting ways.

Sustainability will also be a critical focus for future innovation. The Steel Tycoons have demonstrated that it is possible to achieve industrial progress while minimizing environmental impact. As we face the challenges of climate change and resource depletion, future leaders will need to prioritize sustainable practices and develop new technologies that support a circular economy. By embracing sustainability as a core value, they can ensure that economic growth is compatible with environmental stewardship.

Collaboration will remain a key driver of innovation in the future. The interconnected world created by the Silicon Sheikhs and Steel Tycoons provides a fertile ground for cross-disciplinary and cross-border collaboration. By working together, individuals and organizations can tackle complex global challenges and create solutions that benefit all of humanity. The future of innovation will be characterized by a spirit of cooperation and a shared commitment to creating a better world.

The stories of the Silicon Sheikhs and Steel Tycoons are a testament to the power of vision, determination, and collaboration. Their legacies continue to inspire us to dream big, push the boundaries of what is possible, and create lasting positive change. As we look to the future, we can draw on their examples to guide us on our own journeys of innovation and impact. The next generation of leaders and innovators will build on their foundations, driving progress and shaping a better world for all.

In **"The Silicon Sheikhs and Steel Tycoons: Billionaires Who Built Countries,"** embark on a captivating journey through the lives of visionary entrepreneurs who have reshaped the world. This insightful book delves into the stories of the Silicon Sheikhs, the tech titans who harnessed the power of digital innovation to create global empires, and the Steel Tycoons, the industrial magnates who laid the physical foundations of modern society.

From humble beginnings to monumental successes, these pioneering figures navigated challenges, embraced cutting-edge technologies, and drove societal progress. The book explores their relentless pursuit of excellence, their ability to foresee and capitalize on emerging trends, and their commitment to creating lasting positive change. Through detailed chapters, readers will gain a deeper understanding of how these leaders revolutionized industries, built infrastructure, and fostered global connectivity.

"The Silicon Sheikhs and Steel Tycoons" also highlights the philanthropic endeavors and social impact of these influential individuals. Their dedication to education, healthcare, and environmental sustainability has left an indelible mark on society, inspiring future generations to dream big and push the boundaries of what is possible.

CHAPTER 17: THE FUTURE OF INNOVATION

Rich with anecdotes, lessons, and insights, this book is a tribute to the indomitable spirit of the entrepreneurs who have shaped our world. Whether you're an aspiring entrepreneur, a history enthusiast, or simply curious about the forces that drive progress, "The Silicon Sheikhs and Steel Tycoons" offers a compelling and inspiring read.

www.ingramcontent.com/pod-product-compliance
Lightning Source LLC
LaVergne TN
LVHW010442070526
838199LV00066B/6141